Happy Holidays!

Earth Day

By Rebecca Sabelko

BLASTOFF!
Beginners

BELLWETHER MEDIA
MINNEAPOLIS, MN

Blastoff! Beginners are developed by literacy experts and educators to meet the needs of early readers. These engaging informational texts support young children as they begin reading about their world. Through simple language and high frequency words paired with crisp, colorful photos, Blastoff! Beginners launch young readers into the universe of independent reading.

Blastoff! Universe

Reading Level

Grade K

BLASTOFF! Beginners

Grades 1-3

BLASTOFF! READERS

Grade 4

BLASTOFF! DISCOVERY

Sight Words in This Book 🔍

and	how	other	time	with
day	is	people	to	
eat	it	ride	up	
for	made	the	use	
go	on	they	we	

This edition first published in 2023 by Bellwether Media, Inc.

No part of this publication may be reproduced in whole or in part without written permission of the publisher. For information regarding permission, write to Bellwether Media, Inc., Attention: Permissions Department, 6012 Blue Circle Drive, Minnetonka, MN 55343.

Library of Congress Cataloging-in-Publication Data

Names: Sabelko, Rebecca, author.
Title: Earth Day / by Rebecca Sabelko.
Description: Minneapolis, MN : Bellwether Media, 2023. | Series: Happy holidays! | Includes bibliographical references and index. | Audience: Ages 4-7 | Audience: Grades K-1
Identifiers: LCCN 2022009280 (print) | LCCN 2022009281 (ebook) | ISBN 9781644876770 (library binding) | ISBN 9781648348525 (paperback) | ISBN 9781648347238 (ebook)
Subjects: LCSH: Earth Day--Juvenile literature.
Classification: LCC GE195.5 .S35 2023 (print) | LCC GE195.5 (ebook) | DDC 394.262--dc23/eng/20220224
LC record available at https://lccn.loc.gov/2022009280
LC ebook record available at https://lccn.loc.gov/2022009281

Text copyright © 2023 by Bellwether Media, Inc. BLASTOFF! BEGINNERS and associated logos are trademarks and/or registered trademarks of Bellwether Media, Inc.

Editor: Christina Leaf   Designer: Laura Sowers

Printed in the United States of America, North Mankato, MN.

Table of Contents

It Is Earth Day!   4

Time to Care   6

Love the Earth!   10

Earth Day Facts   22

Glossary   23

To Learn More   24

Index   24

It Is Earth Day!

Time to
plant trees!
It is Earth Day!

Time to Care

Earth Day is
on April 22.
It happens
around the world.

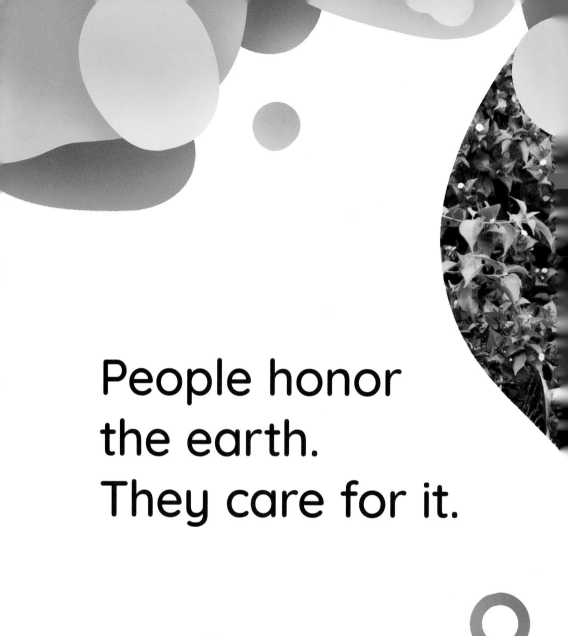

People honor
the earth.
They care for it.

Love the Earth!

People learn
how to **recycle**.

recycling

11

People go outside.
They plant trees
and other plants.

People clean up parks. They pick up **litter**.

litter

People use
less **energy**.
They ride bikes.
They take the bus.

People buy
local foods.
They eat meals
made with plants.

We love and care
for the earth
on Earth Day!

Earth Day Facts

Celebrating Earth Day

plants

local foods

bicycle

Earth Day Activities

learn to recycle

plant plants

use less energy

Glossary

energy

usable power that makes things work

litter

trash and other things that are left on the ground

local

from nearby

recycle

to make new things from used things

To Learn More

ON THE WEB

FACTSURFER

Factsurfer.com gives you a safe, fun way to find more information.

1. Go to www.factsurfer.com.

2. Enter "Earth Day" into the search box and click 🔍.

3. Select your book cover to see a list of related content.

Index

April, 6
bikes, 16
bus, 16
buy, 18
care, 8, 20
clean, 14
earth, 8, 20
eat, 18
energy, 16

foods, 18
learn, 10
litter, 14, 15
local, 18
love, 20
meals, 18
outside, 12
parks, 14
plant, 4, 12, 18

recycle, 10, 11
trees, 4, 12

The images in this book are reproduced through the courtesy of: Alex_Po, front cover; yalayama, p. 3; Prasannapix, pp. 4-5; Denis Kuvaev, pp. 6-7; Lucian Coman, pp. 8-9; Mega Pixel, p. 10; SeventyFour, pp. 10-11; Fotofermer, p. 12; Travelpixs, pp. 12-13; David Pereiras, pp. 14-15; Mongkolchon Akesin, p. 16; Prostockstudio, pp. 16-17; paulista, p. 18; Image Source Trading Ltd., pp. 18-19; Purino, pp. 20-21; Amy Lutz, p. 22; Rawpixel.com, p. 22 (learn to recycle); wavebreakmedia, p. 22 (plant plants); Denis Raev, p. 22 (use less energy); fokke baarssen, p. 23 (energy); Bilanol, p. 23 (litter); Morrell, p. 23 (local); Hurst Photo, p. 23 (recycle).